Turning Risk Into Reward

TurningRISK

Into**REWARD**

Michael McMyne

Entrepreneurs Organization

Turning Risk Into Reward
Michael McMyne

First Edition 2010

Published by Entrepreneurs Organization

Copyright © 2010 Entrepreneurs Organization

Edited by Denise Otillio
Designed by Todd Lape / Lape Designs

Printed in the United States of America.

ISBN 978-0-615-41583-3

This book is dedicated to those individuals who know that the word "risk" begins and the word "success" ends the first sentence of their entrepreneurial story.

CONTENTS

Contents

ACKNOWLEDGMENTS

Producing this project has been a tremendous experience and a labor of love for many individuals who share a common passion for inspiring young entrepreneurs to take a risk in turn for earning a reward. Without their love, passion and unselfishness, this book would not have been possible. While it is not feasible to list them all here, several deserve individual recognition.

First, to Ron and Pam Rubin who have committed to this project from the beginning and saw its powerful impact early on; their generosity has touched so many lives.

Next, we are grateful to our teammates at Entrepreneurs Organization who have partnered with us in so many ways. Specifically, Donna Carrigan whose daily management made working with the students a terrific experience—her energy, follow-through and timely delivery is unmatched! Brian Costanzo, Dean Lindal, and Kevin Langley all teamed up to allow this project to have such broad impact and distribution— we could never have done this without their vision and commitment to advancing the cause of global student entrepreneurship!

Finally, to our editorial and design team: Denise Otillio, our editor, who worked closely with each of our students in the compilation of this book. To Lori Chitwood and Gina Amador of the Republic of Tea who produced our magnificent cover and stayed the course through numerous revisions – they are incredibly talented and gifted and such an important element of our team! Lastly, to Todd Lape of Lape Designs who designed our text on such a crunched timeline!

INTRODUCTION
"Turning Risk into Revenue"

Yellow flags, "Take the turn slowly"; yellow lights, "Be ready to brake"; yellow images, "Life forms crossing the path." Each flag, light, image, warning, amplifies one common message: CAUTION. Most people heed the message and obey. They slow cautiously; brake evenly, and look carefully. Only then, do they proceed. This cautionary strategy is what most people follow.

However, the student entrepreneurs who share their stories in this book are not most people. The major distinguishing factor between these young entrepreneurs and the rest of the more cautious world is that these successful, enterprising young adults did not adopt or confuse a "traffic" philosophy for a life philosophy. For these young adults, the word CAUTION remained nothing more than a wise warning. For these individuals, the word caution did not become a life motto. The word RISK did. More than any other factor, that one syllable philosophy distinguishes the individuals featured in this book from most people. Simply stated, these young men and women took a risk. Stated more accurately, these young entrepreneurs took *the risk.*

At this point, anyone reading this introduction may be asking, "What is the difference?" After all, risk is risk. As these stories will attest, that assumption is wrong. Understanding the difference is critical to appreciating the process that these individuals undertook in order to take their journey of making risk become revenue.

These stories illuminate the business process of individuals who take a risk and who are motivated not by the wish, "I would like to do..." but by the belief, "I must do." Clearly, each story in this book has as its genesis not a wish, but a belief.

As the stories unfold, and the narrators share strategies, challenges, and triumphs, one common theme emerges. The reoccurring theme is that these young talented individuals left nothing to chance. *The risk* is researched, strategized, discussed, revised, reworked, embraced. Somewhere in each story, the young entrepreneur's belief became certainty, and *the risk* became revenue.

—MICHAEL McMYNE

Turning Risk Into Reward

MILUN TESOVIC

At the age of fifteen, following his passion for technology that previously led him to create *MetroLyrics.com,* the world's most popular lyrics company, Milun Tesovic started *MetroLeap Media.*

Tesovic began his entrepreneurial career with an Internet hosting business, but he quickly identified online song lyrics as being an area which had massive potential. To tap into that potential, Tesovic developed a script to create a comprehensive database of song lyrics, sold his hosting business, and began focusing his skills on *MetroLeap Media* and *MetroLyrics.com.*

Today, Tesovic combines his role as CTO of *Metro-Leap Media* with his work as a student at Simon Fraser University in Vancouver, British Columbia. Recently, Tesovic was awarded the *2009 Global Student Entrepreneur of the Year Award* and was recognized on *Billboard's 2009 30-Under-30 List of Entrepreneurs to Watch.* He continues to evolve *MetroLyrics.com* with innovative lyrics, applications and new services.

MetroLeap Media Inc. is considered to be a world leader in the provision of music and entertainment. Its flagship company, *MetroLyrics.com,* is the first lyrics-dedicated site on the internet to provide users with the largest database of licensed, complete, and accurate song lyrics. This global success is due in part to our partnership with *Gracenote,* a leader in global digital entertainment technology.

These partnerships made it possible for *MetroLyrics* to become the most trafficked lyrics' site in the world reaching more than 40 million visitors a month. With over 100 million page views per month, *MetroLyrics* is the third largest music property in the world.

My present role in the company is that of Chief Technical Officer (CTO) of *MetroLeap Media, Inc.* While fulfilling these responsibilities, I am also an undergraduate student pursuing a degree in Business Administration in Entrepreneurship at Simon Fraser University (SFU) which is located in Burnaby B.C., Canada. Pursuing this particular degree allows me to take a range of electives from computer science to accounting which are topics that not only peak my interest, but they also position me for future success in achieving my entrepreneurial goals.

As I recount my present roles of being both the CTO of a successful company and a college undergraduate student living in Canada, I am amazed at my unique journey. My journey to Canada began when I was nine years old. Following conflict in Bosnia, my family left the country looking for a better life. We found Vancouver, B.C., Canada to be very appealing, and, my family applied for immigration in 1995. The process happened quickly. Two months later, we arrived in Canada, and five years later, we were Canadian citizens.

At that time, I had no idea that my immigration from Bosnia to Canada would provide me with both a different perspective and approach to business. This difference is essential to my success. Because of my experiences, I learned how important it is to look out for and to support one another. I also learned to embrace the positive. When I immigrated from Bosnia, my family possessed very few material goods, but we arrived into a country that presented us with possibilities. I appreciated those possibilities. In Canada, everyone has the opportunity to succeed. As an entrepreneur, this experience of leaving one scenario and of arriving into another so completely different offered me a solid foundation for my dreams to become reality.

When I was fifteen, I began working to make my own dreams reality. I had my own Internet hosting company. I started analyzing the sites that peaked people's interest on the web. Many people seemed to gravitate to the music cites. In my research, I discovered that many cities offered music, and many others offered video games, but very few offered song lyrics. My entrepreneurial drive seemed to "kick in" at that time.

I created the website with my own code, and I started a database of music lyrics. It cost nine dollars a month to purchase the domain. From that one creation, my company grew. In 2002, I was joined by business partner Alan Juristovski, and we incorporated the company. Today, we employ sixteen full time employees, and a handful of part time employees and freelancers. In directing the success of my business, assembling a dedicated, supportive, efficient team was my first crucial business decision. Without this team, my business would not have grown quickly or successfully.

The team was assembled, but *Lyrics* was not fully licensed at the time, and we were approaching publishers who were hesitant to talk. Among these publishers was the lingering concern of what would happen to the business when or if they came on board for licensing. Finally, in April 2008, we signed a deal with *Gracenote.* Shortly after, we signed with *Metroleap* who compensates artists and songwriters. This signing was unique in that it was the first licensing structure of its kind. This signing was also important because signing the deal with *Gracenote* allowed *metrolyrics.com* to offer a larger database of complete and accurate song lyrics from major and top independent publishers and a rights payment system that would accurately compensate the artists and publishers for the use of the lyrics.

As the company started to grow, and our first programmer was hired, there came a time where I had to take a risk. This risk involved giving an employee the passwords and other sensitive information he needed in order to perform his job. If mistakes were made, partners could be upset and revenue and traffic could be negatively impacted. Trusting this employee was a make or break decision for me and my business. I understood the scope of what could happen, and the scenario served as a hurdle to overcome. However, it took me very little time before I realized the necessity of trusting this employee, and I began to feel very comfortable with my decision. Building a team is vital, and realizing that I was, "not the smartest guy in the room" meant the company was much better off. Today, I do very little programming, and with the team around me, work is getting done much faster and better than ever before.

Now, I am beginning to really reap the rewards of my work. My work as an entrepreneur has been recognized by the Advancing Canadian Entrepreneurship 2009 Student Entrepreneur competition where I was awarded the national championship title. This recognition gave me the courage to compete in the Entrepreneurs' Organization's 2009 Global Student Entrepreneur Awards (GSEA) program. In the GSEA program, my company competed against thirty-one competitors from eighteen different countries in live competition that took place at the Ewing Kauffman Foundation in Kansas City, Missouri. I placed first in the competition. I have also been recognized as a member of the 2009 Billboard's "Top 30 under 30" and as SFU's Student Entrepreneur of the Year. In addition, *Metroleap* has also been recognized with a "Red Herring Canada Top Fifty Tech" award which seeks out companies around the world that, "will lead the next wave of disruption and innovation."

None of my success would have been possible without my taking risk. I make business decisions carefully, and I check in with my "gut feeling" to make sure that I steer in the right direction. In a sense, I am adverse to taking uncalculated risks. That being said, however, I do believe "to each his own," and I have seen that the higher level of risk involved in a decision can lead to a greater reward on the other side. My advice as an entrepreneur to other entrepreneurs is to consider what risk tolerance you may have. Many may have the capacity to take a higher level of risk, but my personal experience leans toward that of being more adverse to taking quick risks. However, one thing that I truly believe is crucial to success is finding the right people to do the right jobs. This entails everything from forming a good team, to communicating well and motivating individuals to grow together. As a company, we cultivate our teams by taking part in team building exercises. Our aim is to take a team to a point where it gels, and this process can take a few months. We know it is working when we observe the right level of inter-team communication going back and forth. As a company, we were very picky in building our team, understanding that knowledge can be grown and that finding the right personality was most important. I believe that there is more opportunity to build on knowledge than there is opportunity to modify a potential employee's behavior.

My comfort with my risk level, my team, and with positioning my team in the right jobs allows me to enjoy my work. For me, that means doing something different every day. In particular, creating teams and watching a group effort materialize into something for the sake of the company.

From my perspective, what defines an entrepreneur is the impact he/she has in influencing the community, employees, and the business market. To maintain the right positive influence, a question I ask myself is, "Am I doing something malicious to the market or am I improving it?" To answer that question, I take into consideration how I am compensating employees and how I am ensuring that the total influence and impact of our company is beneficial both to the community and to the industry.

I encourage the readers of this book to keep defining your entrepreneurial path and developing your sense of knowledge. Continue growing and having fun at the same time. Consider the importance of communication, an area in which I have struggled. Stay focused on success and building bigger and better teams. Consider build a good team around you that you can rely on. Take care to empower employees and motivate a team that is on the same page. Consider asking, "Where is it we want to go as a team?" Once you have a sure answer, implement this momentum in a proper way so that it is really impacting both the top and bottom line as well as the quality of products and the working atmosphere.

What I hope you take from this chapter would be the key elements which I feel are needed to "turn a risk into reward." Based on my experience, the elements to consider are communication, building a strong team and knowing your own comfort with risk. These three factors will help in determining success as an entrepreneur.

Turning Risk Into Reward

REZA BAVAR

"Risk is a dragon that lives in us all."

—REZA BAVAR

I believe that risk is a primordial urge that is coded into all people before they are even born. Think about it; every second of each day, somewhere, millions of sperm hurl themselves into a "sperm-hostile" environment in the effort to propagate life—to create. With that same urge, each day, every day, somewhere, young entrepreneurs hurl themselves into the unknown for one purpose- to create. For me, this is the definition of the "dragon" of risk.

As I write this chapter, I have three businesses that I have founded: a law practice, Bavar Law Group, my new "passion" business, **Sparx by Bavar,** and a business collaboration that's starting to take shape, a baby product company which as of now remains unnamed.

My law firm is an established business that in a few short years has served hundreds of clients. I have spent these "short years" building relationships that have helped to facilitate the growth of my law firm. For the most part, I have enjoyed the process, but this is not really my passion, and it took the untimely death of a sixteen year old miracle of a human being named Ricardo "Ricky" Resendiz to make me realize this.

As I watched Ricky battle the T-Lymphoblastic Non-Hodgkin's Lymphoma that slowly consumed his body, I found daily inspiration in his strength. He received no less than five rounds of chemotherapy and endured searing pain that I cannot even begin to imagine, but he did it with a grace and gratitude that forever changed how I perceive life and its purpose.

During this time, I had the honor of meeting most of Ricky's family and developed a relationship with them that transcends genealogy—I love them, and they love me. When Ricky passed away, I was one of the first people in his room, and I will never lose the memory of the feeling of love that filled the room. Of course, there was sadness that this portion of Ricky's journey was over, but there was also a palpable appreciation for the life that he lived.

Soon after the beginning of Ricky's new journey, I began my own. I travelled to Queretaro, a historic city in the heart of Mexico to witness yet another miracle—Ricky's funeral. The cathedral, built in the architectural style of Renaissance Europe, was beautiful. At the funeral, the cathedral was filled with well-wishers almost all of whom were dressed completely in white. Outside, there were hundreds of white balloons and white doves. For me, the experience was almost mystical.

In that cathedral, bathed in the light streaming through the windows, I celebrated Ricky's life, and I was given something vital for my journey... Purpose. In some special way, Ricky gave me the courage not just to take risk, but to define it with purpose. I can never thank Ricky or his family enough for inspiring me and for literally breathing new life into my "dragon." You see, prior to Ricky, I had a strong appetite for taking risk, but I never defined the purpose behind the risks I would take. Now, I do.

After I returned to the United States from Mexico, I began to take a very hard look at my life. I became grateful for every experience I ever had in my life, and I realized the foolishness underlying all of my regrets.

I resolved to close my law practice and begin the development of my new company, **Sparx by Bavar**. This is a company that I feel a passion to create because it would enable me to accomplish one of my greatest desires: bringing people together. To accomplish this desire was extremely risky. I sold my car and depleted my savings. With the $50,000 that I was able to gather, I plunged joyfully into **Sparx.** At this point in my business, I am in the process of engineering, designing, and manufacturing electric hookah heads which will make hookah use easier, cleaner, healthier, tastier, and sexier. My goal with **Sparx** is to bring something that is on the fringe—hookah use—into the mainstream.

It is my belief that hookah brings people together and facilitates the exchange of ideas, experiences, and stories, which shift people's perceptions and attitudes. This shift slowly changes the world. I created **Sparx** to change the world, or at least help to facilitate that change—this is my "Dragon's Purpose." Every risk I take now involves my measuring the risk against the purpose in my heart.

Be advised that following your "dragon- risk" will not be applauded by everyone especially your parents. My parents are far from being thrilled with my decision to abandon my law practice in order to create **Sparx.** Frequently, my parents have attempted to tame my "dragon." Believe me, it is hard to see your dad lose sleep over decisions that you have made, but part of being an entrepreneur is uncomfortable—not just for you, but for the people around you. If it were all easy, entrepreneurship would be called the lottery.

Now that **Sparx** is somewhat established, I am pursuing the development of the yet "unnamed baby product company" which, in its own way, will be as innovative as **Sparx.** Creating innovative products allows me to satisfy my insatiable desire to create, and, in the process, change people's lives. I have experienced, first hand, the impact of positive innovation on a person's world view.

I am approaching this new business venture a bit differently partly to assure my dad of a good night's sleep and partly to ensure the success of my new venture. I crafted a business plan that has now been reviewed by a number of successful entrepreneurs some from within and others from outside of the Entrepreneurs' Organization. I intend to use this business plan to expand **Sparx** and to guide the establishment of my yet unnamed baby product company.

In addition to my business plan for **Sparx,** I am actively seeking mentors to help me direct my efforts. My friends and advisors suggest that I seek five mentors, but in keeping with my unique spirit, I might "kick it up a notch" Emeril style and go for six, or I might " kick it down a notch" Boyardee style to three or four. The ideal number is not important, the ideal people are. In my search, I will seek, and I am sure that I will find those wise professionals who will best guide my efforts.

It's somewhat scary to roll the dice in this way, but my "dragon" loves it—the more freedom I give it, the stronger we both become. Sure, there are moments of panic, but the stronger your dragon, the more short-lived these moments will be.

As I journey, I learn that seeking out risk that satisfies your purpose is immensely rewarding. I am having more fun now than I have ever had in my life. What is left of my hair is longer, and I do not have to wear suits. Life is becoming a game—one long game that is contributing to my personal and spiritual growth. Finally, my appetite for risk has exposed me to interesting people. These people are sources of much of my creative energy.

So here I find myself thirty-five years old and penning a new chapter—the most challenging chapter—in the story of my life. My dragon has found its purpose, and we are both happy. The thrill of pursuing something that has personal meaning to me is immeasurable.

Every risk and every challenge that I have had to face because of those risks have been worth the sacrifices that I have had to make—I pray this aspect of my nature never changes.

So what is the purpose of my telling my story? I will answer that question with yet another story. When I was a young man, just barely licensed to drive, my Sufi Master pulled me aside and told me something that has always remained with me... he told me to live life in such a way that when I am dead, I will have taken a piece of this world with me. I pass this advice on to you as a prayer.

I pray that you will live your life in spectacular ways. That you will challenge yourself and revel in the struggles and successes you will, undoubtedly, experience. I pray that you recognize the truth of your own inherent greatness and shout, "I Am" from the highest mountaintops. I pray that you find your purpose and feed your dragon until it can reach any height and burn through any obstacle.

Follow your heart's dreams wherever they may lead you, and let the energy behind all that you accomplish break off a piece of this world for you to take with you!

With Love and Admiration,
Reza Bavar

Turning Risk Into Reward

ANDREA HERRERA

Andrea Herrera is the founder and president of **Amazing Edibles.** The company which began in 1994 caters and hosts private events, and offers cooking classes in a converted 5,000 square foot loft space just west of downtown Chicago. In fifteen years, the company has grown from its original purpose of catering parties and intimate gatherings for individuals and small groups to catering events to accommodate up to 5,000 people for corporate groups including *Harpo Productions, Apple Computer,* and *Deloitte.* **Amazing Edibles** also serves clients in the educational and non-profit sector such as

Catholic Charities, and *Northwestern University.* Ms. Herrera is active in Chicago as a board member for: *Entrepreneurs Organization Chicago Chapter, Cornell College National Alumni Board of Directors, ICNC Industrial Council of Near West Chicago.* Through her involvement with *The Entrepreneur's Organization,* Ms. Herrera is committed to supporting all emerging entrepreneurs, particularly women and minority business owners. Ms. Herrera's son, fourteen year old Jake, is an avid athlete who supports the company by devising marketing strategies.

AMAZING BEGINNINGS

In 1994, I decided to start **Amazing Edibles** using my apartment as the base of operations. I had worked in restaurants since I was thirteen, and although I studied English, music and art history at Cornell College with the ambition of a career in arts administration, my first job after my college graduation was as an assistant manager for a restaurant. After a few years, I was offered a job as a general manager with the Levy Organization where I worked at a number of their properties. During that eight year period, my primary job was as the general manager of *The Rehearsal Room,* the restaurant, bar and concessions services at the Goodman Theater. This particular venue was the Levy Organization's first foray into working with cultural institutions. In my life, this career experience was pivotal in directing my journey because I had a hand in shaping how the company interfaced with cultural institutions. Looking back, I identify that my responsibilities as general manager offered me "on the job" training for my future role as an entrepreneur. As a general manager, I had almost autonomous control over the decision making process as well as the day-to-day running of the operation. However, although I had a great deal of autonomy, I also had a great deal of support and expert advice from a large and successful company. I was lucky.

After leaving the Levy Organization, I took some time to myself to motorcycle cross-country. When I returned to Chicago, I worked again in the food industry. This time I worked as a waitress. The change from endless work days as a general manager to leaving work behind at the end of a shift as a waitress, turned out to be just what I needed to recharge. Soon, I found myself thinking of opening my own company. My own company would allow me to put all of my hard work and energy into something that was my own. So, beginning my own company is what I did. I had the good fortune of being able to ease into entrepreneurship with a high level of support from my friends and family, including a generous gift of seed money from my parents. In addition to that emotional and financial support, my business background had exposed me to some of the challenges that I would be facing as a small business owner. My previous experience and preparation allowed me to grow steadily from the outset. In 1995, I was in a position to expand into a rented 1,000 square foot storefront that I outfitted to meet my company's needs. I positioned myself for success.

I soon found myself successfully making a comfortable living, and my business was growing steadily. With a confidence born of success, and without the burden of debt, I assembled a knowledgeable creative team. Together we went about building a solid reputation that included ongoing relationships with corporate clients such as *LaSalle Bank, AON,* and *Nike.* My company continued to expand, and its operation ran smoothly until 9/11. From that moment, my world shifted dramatically.

For the first time since the business began, the phones stopped ringing. Business tumbled, and sales dropped from $500,000 in sales each year with steadily growing profits to being down 50% almost overnight. Individual clients stopped entertaining catered events. In a move to curtail catering costs, corporate clients, who were now a huge market for us, began holding either mid-morning or late- afternoon meetings rather than day-long professional development activities. This reduction in demand was an unique experience for **Amazing Edibles,** and it forced me to think more strategically about the business rather than simply to want its success. Up to this point, planning strategically was not something I had done. I was caught in the aftershocks of an event that played out in ways I could never even have imagined, and those events led me down the path to the biggest risk I would take in my business. I bought a permanent kitchen space.

By the time the holiday season rolled around, usually a busy, bustling one for any catering business, the majority of our corporate clients had decided to cancel their office holiday parties and donate the money that they would have spent to charities. As the trend continued into the spring, it became clear that corporate sales would remain stunted, so I picked myself up and refocused on a new market, that of non-profit and educational institutions. Because of my expert staff, I was able to take on a more prominent marketing and sales role. I called on prospective clients directly to promote **Amazing Edibles** as an option for their catered events. My sales calls included offering free catered lunches to give them a "taste " of the quality meal they could expect from us, and my strategy worked. Our new clients included The *University of Chicago, The University of Illinois at Chicago, Cicero Public Schools,* and *The United States Army;* existing relationships with the *Chicago Public Schools* and the city of Chicago also grew tremendously. This strategy was a push that paid off. Non-profit and educational institutions now make up about 70% of my business.

Slowly, business picked up, and five years later, with $600,000 in annual sales, I found myself bursting at the seams in my 1,000 square foot storefront. **Amazing Edibles** was ready for expansion and growth, so I decided to take the plunge and purchase my own space. I knew I was ready.

AMAZING RISK

At the very beginning, my only plan was to start my own business and make it successful. I knew that I would not approach this venture in the same way that I had approached all my previous ventures- intuitively. I would always forge ahead, work hard, and by force of will, I would make things happen. While entering into any business venture involves risk, to a certain degree, my business ventures had been charmed and cushioned by the fabulous support of people I loved. My mindset is now different. I wanted to take myself more seriously as an entrepreneur and as a leader. I needed to approach business differently because purchasing my own business space is a risk I knew needed to be approached with a bit more calculation.

In 2006, when I decided to buy my own space, I made an official business plan, and I started the process of looking for a new space. I was idealistic and perhaps naïve as I began my search. I had a couple of numbers in my head: $300,000 to purchase a property and $100,000 to renovate it. However, I had not factored in the costs for permits or licenses, but I moved ahead confidently. A year later, I found my new home, 5,000 square feet of completely raw space. It had no plumbing, very little electric, just bricks and concrete. The space would require a complete build out to meet the needs of **Amazing Edibles.** Since I could picture myself in this space, I needed to replace my previous numbers with two new numbers: $400,000 and $300,000. The former would be my new purchase price, and the latter would be my construction and equipment costs. This 100-year old loft in a neighborhood adjacent to downtown Chicago where most of my clients were located would give me parking, more storage for dry goods, and walk-in freezers and refrigerators. It was a place that would allow me to give higher quality service to my clients and create a safer, more comfortable, and productive environment for my employees. I reworked the numbers, and I began the process of buying my space. Even though the price would leave me virtually penniless, I was exhilarated by the thought of my business being in its own space, and this was the perfect space.

Unfazed by problems with the financing at the eleventh hour, I closed on the property in July 2007. Soon after, I began anticipating our busiest holiday season ever. I also anticipated that the space would be finished, and **Amazing Edibles** would be in its new home before the season even started. Soon, serious problems with the contractor surfaced, and by the time I became fully aware of the contractor's fraud, I had already purchased all the equipment for the space, hired new employees, and given the contractor all of the money we had agreed on to finish the job. He did not finish.

I finally came to terms with the embarrassment related to the situation with my former contractor, pulled myself together and recruited staff, family and friends and a few professionals, and we finished the necessary work over a three-day weekend that had been left unfinished by the contractor for over a month. **Amazing Edibles** moved into its beautiful new home on January 1, 2008. The move from a 1,000 to 5,000 square foot space allowed me to purchase eight stoves, grills and fryers, and of course, install walk-in freezers and refrigerators. The additional storage and cold space meant that my team could keep costs down by keeping ingredients on hand allowing us to expand our customer base and serve them more efficiently. The new space also allowed me to add additional services such as hosting on site events and offering cooking classes. At the same time, I realized that I should be negotiating a new mortgage agreement. I finalized the new loan in September 2008, just weeks before the stock market crash and subsequent financial crisis ensued.

Quite honestly, the decision and subsequent risk I took to find a permanent home for **Amazing Edibles** was, for me, an important step in my growth as a businesswoman. After twelve years of being fairly isolated in my business and having my nose to the proverbial grindstone, researching physical spaces opened my eyes to other resources available to me as a businesswoman. It also connected me to people and groups which have become invaluable to me at this stage of expanding and maintaining my business. By reaching out and observing what was happening with businesses in Chicago, I became a better manager to my team, and I discovered that there were new and different ways to accomplish my goal that could make my life easier as an entrepreneur.

I also reached out to the larger community to share my experiences. I joined the boards of three organizations: *Cornell College National Alumni Board of Directors, The Industrial Council of Near West Chicago,* and *The Professional Partners Board of A Children's Place.* I connected with the city as a businesswoman and became involved in the Entrepreneurs Organization (E.O.) through admission to the accelerator program. With E.O., I discovered a new level of support that was different from that of friends and family. This was the support of a group of dynamic entrepreneurs who had practical knowledge about how I could make my business better. Among the group, I found mentors and colleagues with whom I could share my own experiences in an environment that fostered mutual growth. Through the program, I feel I earned the equivalent of an MBA, and with the program's network of support, I accelerated my business and exceeded one million dollars in revenue for the first time. Perhaps most importantly, I began to realize that the story of my entrepreneurial journey could be of value to someone else.

AMAZING CONCLUSIONS

I believe that in addition to having an unshakable belief in one's success, the ability to change and to take risks is perhaps the most important quality that any entrepreneur can have. As in other areas in life, without these two qualities there can be no growth. All of this has helped me reach an elite level of businesses that can claim one million dollars in sales each year.

I know that I never could have reached this benchmark by simply continuing to work hard. In addition to hard work, idealism, giving back, and risk taking are all a part of the entrepreneurial experience. Although each one of these characteristics has a place in my success, it is my willingness to take a risk that opened my eyes to new possibilities and broadened my experience. Most importantly, risk forced me to meet the challenges that I might never have met, and as any entrepreneur will tell you, anticipating growth and meeting challenge are what define a business.

Turning Risk Into Reward

LAWRENCE KIM TZE WEN

Lawrence KIM Tze Wen was born on March 12, 1982, in Singapore. After completing middle school, he attended Singapore Polytechnic where he was awarded his degree in Banking and Financial Services. He continued his academic career at Singapore Management University where he graduated in 2009 with a Bachelor in Business Management with an emphasis in Business Law.

When Lawrence KIM was seventeen years old, he began his entrepreneurial career in the print industry. That early experience ignited his creative drive and guided him into a variety of other business ventures including the launching of his current inspection company, **Ebenezer NDT Services and Elizer** where he serves as the company's Managing Director.

In addition to his management responsibilities, Lawrence KIM serves in a variety of civic leadership roles including *Young Business Leader (NYC), Honorary Treasurer of the School Advisory Council* ,and *The Non-Destructive-Testing Society of Singapore.*

In the course of his career, Lawrence KIM's leadership in both the business and the civic community has been recognized and awarded. In 2009, he was named 2nd Runner Up for GSEA's *Lessons from the Edge Award.* Previous to that honor, he won the highest recognition at the *SMU Innovations Competition*, and he received nomination for the *National Youth Award,* the *Spirit of Enterprise Award* and the *IDA Innovations Award.* In addition, Lawrence KIM is the recipient of the *ETDF Funding* and *ICS* which are both under the direction

of the Spring Singapore and Economic Development
Board.

"Only time can prove how much you love someone." This quotation can easily be transferred to the
entrepreneur who has begun the journey of beginning
his/her own business. I have experienced the truth of
this quotation in the relationship I have with my own
business, and I have learned that only time can prove
how much one can grow to love the challenge and
adventure of being an entrepreneur and of developing a relationship with a growing, changing, successful
business. Since 1999, my business has become a driving passion in my life that has taken me on a journey
of challenge and triumph, and as my business grew
and changed, so have I. I began and remained on this
entrepreneurial journey because of one word: AGAPE,
a Greek term which translated means, "sacrificial love."
Through Agape, I have been able to overcome the challenges and celebrate the triumphs of being a business
owner. However, many factors contribute to the success of this sacrificial love. In this chapter, I will share

what I have come to understand about the components that I have discovered to be most important.

TIME

The early stage of building a business requires a great commitment of time. Initially, during the first months, sometimes years, the majority of your time will be spent running your business. If your experience is anything like my own, seldom will you be thinking of the rewards or the returns. In fact, during most of the hours you will not be thinking; you will be doing and giving. Unlike having **a** job working in a business, having **the** job of running a business requires more than clocking in eight hour shifts, going home, and forgetting about the day's work until the next day. When you own a business, you have to give all that you have and give your best. I worked whatever hours were necessary in the business doing whatever was necessary for the business. I performed the various jobs that being a business owner entails. In addition, I became the salesman, the driver, the hiring manager, and the trainer. The hours of the day were spent on running the business, not on thinking about the returns. Ironically, because of my sacrifice of TIME, and because no conditions were placed on this time, the returns came in abundance.

SELFLESS

Putting the well-being of others before your own is a very noble concept. As a business owner, that concept must become an action. Under any circumstance, the well-being and best interest of the business must come before your own self-interest. As we move away from the early stage of the entrepreneurial journey, there are times when decisions have to be made regarding what to let go or relinquish. For example, when the company has no other profits except the initial investment monies contributed by the entrepreneurs, the decision about how to distribute the money is not complicated. The entire amount is invested for the purpose of growing the business. On the other hand, when the business begins to generate profits, the business owner has to choose between spending the money to reward himself/herself or investing the money back into working capital in order to grow the business. The temptation to do the former is great. However, AGAPE, sacrifice, demands the latter choice.

Sacrifices of this nature are demanded as the company or business continues to grow, and difficult choices must be made. One guiding principle makes the decision much more obvious. A true entrepreneur must focus on the satisfaction of the customers rather than on the increase of his/her profits. The entrepreneur continually operates from the mode of giving back to the larger community specifically to his/her customers.

I cannot dispute the fact that when I first started the business, I was all profit-oriented. I thought that having a business was the only way to bring me out of poverty and the fastest way to make me rich. However, as I matured, my attitude changed. The realization that I have come to as an entrepreneur is that the more I focus on my customers and my product, the more I put quality before cost. That shift in my focus greatly improves my business. I concentrate on developing a business model that delivers the best quality, and I continually study how to deliver this high quality product at the lowest possible cost. Profits follow this shift in attitude.

An entrepreneur is bold and ambitious, striving to build his/her businesses beyond its current stage. He/she seeks to make the most of the business's potential, and he/she understands that in order to do this, the focus must always be not on profit, but on success. Only a spirit of selflessness will bring him/her closer to that goal.

DELIVERING EFFICIENCY

The motto that drives the *Fed-Ex* company to excellence is a motto that all companies could benefit from heeding, "We live to deliver." It does not matter if the product is technology, service, food, or tourism, the urgency must always remain the same: to deliver a consistently high quality product that meets or even exceeds the customers' expectations. In a highly charged competitive business environment, the risk of failing to deliver is always a risk to be taken seriously, and a risk to avoid.

FINAL WORDS

Risk can be greatly reduced by trusting yourself and getting involved in all areas of your business. You may be familiar with the saying that it is better for people to become a "Jack of all trades, but a master of none." I beg to defer. An entrepreneur needs to strive to know everything about his business and master everything that is involved in his business. Entrepreneurs seek their own answers. In fact, this is how an entrepreneur learns best. Finally, I will offer you one final thought to assure you of both personal and business success, "Be true to yourself, and love your business!"

Turning Risk Into Reward

CRAIG MARTYN

ENTREPRENEURSHIP
Risk. Money. Happiness. Life...

Entrepreneurship is something an individual MAKES happen. Hard work, undying passion, innovative ideas— each of these criteria is vital to one's journey toward successful entrepreneurship. However, in addition to work, passion and innovation, one wonders if there is some criteria that is even more integral in leading one through the perils and obstacles of entrepreneurial leadership and away from the complacency and safety of passive mediocrity. To the individuals who have already taken the journey, the answer is obvious. Each would respond with some version of the phrase, "taking the risk." When an entrepreneur defines his or her passion, values, and goals, he or she will have also determined how to take the risk, and, with that assessment, the entrepreneurial journey will have already begun. My hope with this chapter is that you will understand the underlying principles that I followed in my emerging, but already successful entrepreneurial journey.

WHAT IS PASSION?

Passion cannot be ignored. Passion not only defines the individual entrepreneur, it also unites him or her with others who have that same entrepreneurial spirit and drive. In fact, passion is the one characteristic that is shared by every entrepreneur. Do not misunderstand me; I am NOT talking about a passion for money or possessions—very few successful entrepreneurs are motivated solely by material gain. I am talking about the passion that allows an individual to become an expert at something, define obstacles, create solutions, and help others through the knowledge that he or she has gained.

I have experienced such passion in my own life. From a young age, I had a passion for trains. I have never discovered why I had this particular passion, but the "why" does not matter. What matters is that I could not ignore it. I watched trains; I rode them; I read about them; I collected them. I became a young expert on modern North American railroading. As I grew older, I not only possessed an expertise on railroading, I also had developed a keen sense for business. Soon "it" hit me! Why not combine my passion for trains with my sense for business? I did, and **BLMA Models** was born...

DEFINE YOURSELF

It does not take very long into a college freshman's academic career before he/she recognizes the degree program that either holds the most interest for him/ her, or, on the other hand, that requires the least effort from him/her. Typically, that recognition is the litmus test for a future career. Just as typically, the individual who pursues a career and a future based on only that "test" will soon be depleted of a source of creative energy.

To avoid this scenario, my advice is first to ask yourself the question, "Who am I?" Your answer to that question will propel you to finding a career path based on your own passion. You will discover what you love doing and not simply what you are "good at doing." Next, you must pursue that passion. Take the initiative...take the risk. Successful entrepreneurs do this. You will find that once you are engaged with your passion, your love will energize your work ethic and push your creativity "through the roof!" Success will not always come easy, but what is life without challenges, and triumphs and risks?

DO MORE

Entrepreneurs are do-ers! Literally, NOTHING will happen unless the entrepreneur makes it happen.

When it was my turn to make "it" happen, I developed instincts, learned programs, and interpreted jargon; I met, questioned and listened to influential individuals who were respected in their fields. In addition, in order to maintain high business standards, keep costs down, and focus on my vision, I did anything that was necessary for me to become proficient in the knowledge and skills which were essential for my business to become successful. For example, I gained expertise in various computer programs including *2D CAD Design* and *Graphic Design*. I did whatever it took. As a result, my business gained value, and my brand gained credibility among employees, vendors and customers.

Making "it" happen does not only pertain to the knowledge that you have working for you, but also, and more importantly, to the persons you have working for you. Hiring the BEST person for a position is crucial, but you must also ensure that the personal values of that individual are aligned with your own personal and business values and ethics. When evaluating employees, I ask difficult, probing questions such as, "What is the single biggest misconception about yourself?" and "If money wasn't an object, what would be your ideal legacy on this earth?" A great deal of a business's success depends on a potential employee's answer to such questions. Therefore, you must align yourself with those individuals who share your attitude, values, and core beliefs.

ASK
Why?

As an entrepreneur, the greatest reward you will have is in developing your own path to success. On this path, you will, no doubt, have to tackle many difficult situations. Leadership and creativity emerge in these challenging situations. However, initially, young entrepreneurs do not realize this fact. When approached with a problem, their first response is to seek their solution in what other business leaders had done in similar circumstances. My advice to you is to avoid this strategy. Sure, examine previous solutions, but then," think outside of the box." Take your risk; be innovative. Ask," WHY?" Why does something have to continue to be done in a certain way? Why has it been done like *that* for so long? Finally, you may ask," Why can't we change things?" If you have no answer to that question, then, you are thinking like an entrepreneur. My next advice to you is to take the risk; walk your path.

BUSINESS FUNDAMENTALS
Thoughts for a successful personal and business life.

Communication—The ability to communicate effectively may be the single most important factor in business. Effective communicators are able to share their vision, motivate their supporters and accomplish their goals. In my efforts to communicate, I regularly step back and think about a simple question: What is my point, and how can I effectively communicate this message to my audience. Whether I am addressing marketing staff, sales professionals, or my own family, I make certain that I am doing a good job of explaining my point as it pertains to my audience.

Quality—The quest for quality should permeate every detail of your business. Every little detail of your business contributes to its overall success. Therefore, establishing high standards for quality must motivate every decision you make. Quality should define not only your product or service, but also its packaging, its website, the photos on the website, etc., etc. My point is to set your standards as high as possible – this really is up to you!

Persistence—Never give up. Those entrepreneurs who keep focused on their strengths are the entrepreneurs who accomplish their goals over time. Through tough times, keep your focus. Build on your strengths. In building a successful business, hard work cannot be replaced.

Attitude—Surround yourself by people with positive attitudes. Aspire to the highest levels you can, and do not allow small issues to block your way. If you are positively motivated and happy, success will come as long as you put your efforts into productive ideas. Negative ideas are counter -productive, so avoid them at all costs.

Values—You must develop a core set of values on which you base your personal and business decisions. To some extent, the saying, "Business is business" is true. However, it is people who make up a business. My values of honesty, integrity, friendship, kindness, fairness and reliability, determine how I interact with all of the individuals who are involved in my business.

Mentors—To be honest, I have lazy moments, and I wish I could stay within my comfort zone. However, I soon come to realize that for business, a comfort zone can be a deadly zone. Whenever, I feel the temptation to remain comfortable, I seek out a mentor. I cannot stress enough that mentors will exponentially help grow your business and enhance your personal life – that is, if you interact with them effectively: phone a mentor frequently; send emails, or set-up lunch dates.

A mentor's advice, as well as your interest in seeking his/her advice and insight are essential to your keeping motivated.

Cash Flow—As a business grows, you will have slight positive and negative shifts in cash flow. When you realize your first negative cash flow, do not panic. Depending on the size of your business, your cash flow can fluctuate one-hundred thousand dollars or more in a single month. In such a situation, continue to smartly and confidently grow your business. Remain attentive, spend wisely, and plan for the expected... and unexpected.

THE BOTTOM LINE

There are a million ways to find your success. The ideas I have presented here are my own; they have worked for me. You must absorb everything you hear; digest the information, and create your own destiny. The major point is to be true to yourself, and you will LOVE what you do – the rest will fall into place naturally. Lastly, hold on tight; entrepreneurship is a wild ride!

Turning Risk Into Reward

MUNYARADZI SHADAYA

A passionate marketer and brand engineer, Munyaradzi Shadaya is the founder and CEO of **IMPETUS GLOBAL LTD,** a marketing consulting business.

Previous to **IMPETUS GLOBAL LTD**, Munyaradzi Shadaya, at the age of eighteen, ran the day to day operations of **SUPAWASH**, a soap manufacturing business. Here, the particular emphasis was on sales. Three years later, in October of 2008, the concept for **IMPETUS** came to Munyaradzi Shadaya in a dream, and, Munyaradzi Shadaya, "has been living this dream ever since."

A gifted entrepreneur in many areas, Munyaradzi Shadaya identifies his greatest gift as being his ability to be innovative in addressing the challenges of his clients. An example of this innovation is his creation of **Brand Diligence,** a tool that is still being used exclusively at **IMPETUS** worldwide.

A priority for Munyaradzi Shadaya is integrating his Christian faith into his corporate and social entrepreneurship career. Munyaradzi Shadaya has been successful in establishing this priority. He was named national winner of the *Global Students Entrepreneur Awards (GSEA)*. He was also a GSEA global finalist in 2009.

MY RISK....THE RISK OF FAILURE!

The Oxford Dictionary defines risk as "exposure to danger or loss." In this definition, the key words for me are "danger" and "loss." When going into business, an individual faces taking countless risks; however, some are feared more than others. For me, the risk that I fear most is the fear of FAILURE. Very early in my entrepreneurial career, I was exposed to this risk. A myriad of issues and situations could trigger failure for me at anytime:

- The first situation that could trigger failure was my age. I was only 21 when I started IMPETUS. My youth gave me little credibility to potential clients. For them, my age translated to a lack of maturity and an inability to deal with any marketing problems.
- I had no convincing skills, expertise, or proven track record. I did not hold any ideal academic qualification which would allow for a smooth penetration into the market.
- I had no capital. I had very little cash savings from my previous businesses, and these could not even suffice to buy office fixtures. My available cash could only support three months of providing the basic overheads.

- I had no team support or business structure in place that could add the intellectual capital which was needed to run the business "professionally."
- I was involved with a high risk project. The wide scope of services that we were to provide would involve massive marketing programs that carried a huge financial risk for clients.
- My company would face fierce competition from large and established visual marketing companies.
- The economy in which I would launch my project was battered, and marketing projects such as the my own are considered as being unnecessary luxuries in my country of Zimbabwe.

The above factors contributed to a very low level of confidence in **IMPETUS**, my marketing consulting firm. Because **IMPETUS** is my company and I have the spirit of an entrepreneur, I immediately sought ways in which I could lessen the risk that the factors presented for the start-up of my company. Eventually, we confronted the risk, and **IMPETUS** is now recognized as being, "The world's largest and best marketing consultancy."

In taking the risk, I faced many challenges. The first involved learning to balance the many phases of my life activities. As a critical part-fulfillment of my studies at the University of Zimbabwe, I had just begun my undergraduate internship at a very reputable local firm. The minimum duration of the program was eight full months. Both the business and the studies were critical components for my future career. However, also critical to my future was my emerging business. Because both of these responsibilities were very important to me, I had to devise a plan to effectively handle both. My first strategic move was to strike a balance. During the day, I performed my academic requirements that would fulfill my internship. At night and on weekends, I performed my business obligations. After completing my internship, I embraced being a full time entrepreneur.

HOW I WENT ON

The risk I had of failing was a constant and strong presence inside of me. However, my desire to develop a thriving successful business which could contribute to my community was more constant and more strong than any fear I had, so I began my journey. After doing an inventory, I identified my assets and possible strategies which I highlighted below:

God—I knew that God was on my side, and I would not fail unless I made the decision to fail. From the very beginning, I decided that no matter what challenges I would meet, failure would never be an option. I simply said, "NO" to failure. One reason for my faith and confidence is the way in which I developed the idea for my company. The idea for my company IMPETUS was given to me in a dream. After several months of praying for some way that I could develop a business, one night, soon after prayer, the idea for a marketing consulting business came to me in a dream, and that was it! I knew from that point on, I would begin taking care of the business of building my business. I could not fail; I could only PROSPER! Even today whenever I feel overwhelmed, this dream has been my single greatest source of inspiration. I reflect on my dream, and I pull myself up again to work on developing the, "greatest business in the world."

I love my work—My business defines my lifestyle, and marketing my business is not work, but comes very naturally to me. Because it is such a natural and creative flow, I enjoy working long hours without feeling drained or worn down. In fact, my work energized me and helped me to manage the long and tedious stretches during the first year of our operation. I remember whenever we were marketing the *Brand Diligence* contract, my working day would average 20 hours. However, these endless days were not a strain. I really loved everything about the process. A combination of this hard work and passion for the job has made our clients appreciate the **IMPETUS** style of excellence and commitment.

I can create—I have used my God given creative mind to invent unique consulting tools. Of note here is the

Brand Diligence tool which is a comprehensive internal brand audit tool. This tool integrates a business' internal processes, people and systems. This tool is based on understanding that the interaction of these three variables embodies the brand that the stakeholders are going to experience. *Brand Diligence* took the market by storm and gave IMPETUS credibility. The first *Brand Diligence* was on the fast track to being retailed.

Mentors—Before considering this business, I had formed close relationships with mentors. I gained wisdom from listening to the stories of the mentors who had been successful in business. Before I met my mentors, I acknowledged the fact that I was young and prone to making mistakes that were associated with inexperience. I also realized my limited knowledge in some areas, as well as my immaturity in making certain business decisions especially when I would be undertaking some complex marketing operations. To guide me through these challenges, I had three formal mentors. However, I also had numerous informal mentors who never knew that through their stories and conversations, they were mentoring me. From all of my mentors, I learned what I wanted and did not want for my life. In some instances, I have not agreed with their methods, but still, I have learned lessons.

In addition to physical mentors, I have experienced the wisdom of virtual mentors. My virtual mentors have been a real source of inspiration for me especially during time of immense pressure and adversity. They have kept me going. My main virtual mentors are Strive Masiyiwa, Nigel Chanakira, and Douglas Mamvura. What particularly inspires me about these individuals is that they have managed to integrate their Christian faith with their mind for business, and a heart for the world. They live very close to home and make me believe in myself even stronger. I am privileged now to have Doulas Mamvura not only as my virtual mentor, but also as my physical mentor.

Without a doubt, mentors play a significant role in eliminating a young entrepreneur's fear of taking a risk and failing in the process. From personal experience, I know that to be true.

A Board of Directors—Because I was about to start running a business, I had to start assembling a structure that would support and help direct the efforts of laying the foundation. I began by forming a strong board of directors. These individuals would provide strategic impetus to the business by reviewing my strategy proposals, business performance, mentoring, and networking. In addition, the board would boost my self-confidence as well as the confidence that my clients had in me.

As I was assembling my board, I was about to make a very big mistake that could have frustrated this effort. I had proposed a board that consisted of some of the most respected and successful local businessmen and women with whom I had built relationships. What I did not consider was that since these individuals also held positions on boards of other major companies, there could be a conflict of interest with my own company. If this were the case, my business could be harmed more than it could be helped. One of my advisors suggested that I create another type of structure. Following that advice, instead of assembling a board of directors, I assembled a board of advisors.

Advisory Team—Owing to the wise counsel I had received, I created the advisory team.. This group is comprised of individuals representing a cross-section of skills and backgrounds. However, the group does have a common denominator, the astonishing wisdom gathered from years of experience in business either as entrepreneurs or professionals. Through their guidance, I am able to carry myself confidently in leading **IMPETUS** regardless of my inexperience and youth.

Have an accountability partner—The idea of being "my own boss" was fascinating, but being my own boss could have just as easily triggered unnecessary problems. I realized that for the good of my company, I had to become accountable to someone other than my advisory board. I had to also be accountable to someone for the business' day to day operation. It did not take me long to identify the person who would best hold me accountable. My dad was just the man for that job! Like an interested friend, he calls me almost every day to get a progress report. Being able to give a positive report to him is the incentive I need to move forward and make progress. Though he is unaware of it, I converted him into my virtual "boss." To this day, he remains my "boss," and by requesting a progress report, he energizes me to keep making tangible advances in all my endeavors.

Create time everyday to think and reflect adequately—A member of my advisory board gave a word of advice that has become very important to my own well-being. She told me to create time in my day to reflect in quiet. Each day, I manage to create this time of quiet. Without a crowd around, we tend to become real with ourselves, and when we make a choice to be brutally honest with ourselves, we can make the honest decisions that will benefit our business.

Humility—Service business is about serving clients with humility. During the first year of operation, we offered our services either at no cost or at very deep discounts. This strategy was meant to allow our clients to recuperate from the near economic collapse that my country had faced for a number of years. This strategy also enabled us to create the capacity to pay for our services in future years and to establish marketing as being a necessary service in a nation that once viewed it as a luxury.

Networking—During my years at the University of Zimbabwe, I was the head of marketing for a student organization, SIFE. In that capacity, I learned the importance of networking. I have one simple observation about this dynamic. Networking is vital for the growth of any business.

I did not develop this list of these ten essential points in one day. It took me months to generate this list, and I made countless mistakes in my journey. The mistakes became my business lessons and helped me develop "a go forward attitude" which allows me to take life step by step. Even though each step may involve a risk, without taking those steps, IMPETUS would not have become the successful business that it is, nor would it have been recognized for its success.

In October 2009, the Global Student Entrepreneur Awards (GSEA) named me the 2009 GSEA National Champion for Zimbabwe. The following month, I represented Zimbabwe at the thematic GSEA Global Finals in Kansas City, Missouri. I felt like I was beginning to get rewarded for just taking the risk and running with it. On the other hand, because of the awards and recognition that were given to me, I feel that I have much more to lose if I were to fail at any point in my business venture. Am I afraid? Yes. Yet, just as I experienced at the beginning of this entrepreneurial journey, more than fearful, I am invigorated, confident and ready to lead IMPETUS to become, "The World's Biggest and Best Marketing Consulting Business." What greater reward could I have sought?

Turning Risk Into Reward

BRAYDEN OLSON

"The buzz around (Brayden) is that he might well be Seattle's

next Bill Gates or Howard Schultz. No pressure, though."

—XCONOMY.COM

Brayden has built **Novel, Inc**. from a single person company in a dorm room to a twenty person venture backed startup in Seattle, Washington. The company has been featured in *The New York Times*, *Business-Week* and *Xconomy* as well as being the recipient of multiple accolades and global awards.

Among these, **Novel** was selected by *Entrepreneurs' Organization* as the student run enterprise of the year for the Pacific Northwest in 2009, and one of the top 30 such enterprises in the world in the *Global Student Entrepreneur Awards.* In this same competition, **Novel** also received the *Pacific Northwest Innovation Award* from *Microsoft* because of **Novel's** orientation and strategy to revolutionize the video game industry.

Bill George, Professor of Management at Harvard Business School and one of PBS's *Top 25 Business Leaders* of *the Past 25 Years,* says of Brayden, "I am absolutely convinced this young man will do staggering things within his lifetime." Bill George is the CEO who grew **Medtronic** into the world's largest medical technology company and author of the *Business Week* best-sellers *True North* and *Authentic Leadership.*

Although there are a number of great locations in the United States to launch an innovative game studio, Seattle, Washington is the best and the most active for this industry. Yet, even in Seattle, it is noteworthy when a twenty-two year old is the one who is set to launch.

The last time such a young entrepreneur took such a risk was a decade ago when John Vechey launched *PopCap* games. Beating the odds ten years later would be a challenge. Who would seriously consider taking that kind of risk? I would. My name is Brayden Olson, and I am a 22 year old entrepreneur building an innovative videogame company in Seattle.

As any entrepreneur can tell you, skepticism has been on the rise for the last decade. Since the "dotcom bubble," 9/11, and the 2007 stock market crash, the familiar capitalist drive of "greed" has been overshadowed by fear. Businesses have gotten simpler. Investors began to focus on business models that could secure revenue before money needs to be raised. In general, this focus tends to promote businesses that are born of one well-timed clever idea.

Clever business ventures can evolve quickly, but, if cleverness becomes the criteria for a business success, the world may never again see another *Microsoft*. Instead, we can anticipate low risk, high reward, quick payout businesses. For many entrepreneurs, this picture is a real temptation. However, other highly motivated young entrepreneurs still fundamentally believe that a true business is not born of cleverness, but of creativity, passion, hard work and time. These values ignite the world-changing, infrastructure-level innovations that build long term credibility and commitment. I am one of these other highly motivated entrepreneurs who recognize that it will take time to build and perfect my business and that this difficult business model has also proven to be the most rewarding.

Since I was thirteen years old, I wanted to fundamentally innovate the videogame industry. While I never really had any apprehension about starting my business, my first roadblock was arriving at the realization that being an entrepreneur was even an option. I have no history of entrepreneurship in my immediate family, nor had I ever met an entrepreneur as I was growing up. Therefore, up until college, I thought the only way to launch a business would be through joining a company, working my way up and then attempting to make a difference. My thinking at the time was quite reasonable and also quite wrong.

While common sense led me to believe that I needed experience before being an entrepreneur, or making an impact on the world, the evidence contradicted my common sense. All of the technology giants of the world, *Amazon, Apple, Dell, Ebay, Google, Microsoft, Oracle, Yahoo* and *Facebook* were founded by individuals thirty years old or younger.[1] The young entrepreneurs who launched these companies certainly affirmed George Bernard Shaw's observation, "The reasonable man adapt himself to the world; the unreasonable one persists in trying to adapt the world to himself. Therefore all progress depends on the unreasonable man." These companies and others that are successful have become successful because of creative individuals who were too unreasonable to wait. They did not work for a company; they did not become part of corporate America. They had a vision, and they became entrepreneurs.

You will never quite hear the real story of a young entrepreneur's real beginnings. It is always in the best interest of the company to report on what went well rather than to discuss what went poorly. For instance, Bill Gates first product was called *Traf-O-Data*, which was a roadway traffic counter tool designed for helping traffic engineers. It produced a few thousand dollars of revenue. You almost never hear of this device now, but with this product Gates gained critical experience in his journey towards *Microsoft.*

In addition to such small beginnings, there are always upsets, failures, and mistakes. The process always take longer than you think it should. Often countless hours have been logged before a company incorporates, assembles the right team, or refines the version of the idea that they finally take to market. All of this work and the company has just begun.

I am offering those reflections based on my own experience. I started **Novel** in college, made numerous mistakes and spent a great deal of time refining my vision, idea and team. I completed this process before I was expected to have a traditional career. Had I waited even another six months to begin, I may have delayed the launch of **Novel** by years because of the demands that would have come from my being involved in another career.

Of course, being an entrepreneur does have its own set of challenges. The major initial challenges I faced were those I had already overcome: assembling the right team. To be the right team, these individuals each had to have more experience than I had in business. Next, the team and I needed to raise capital in a market where less than 2% of businesses acquire venture capital.[2] I had solutions, but my solution to these problems may not be what you expect.

Both of these challenges and those I continued to meet along the way were not in my control. In the simplest sense, I could not work any harder than I did to find the right team or to get venture capital. In tackling obstacles like these, that cannot be controlled, there is a lesson to learn from Reinhold Niebuhr, who said, "Grace (is needed) to accept with serenity the things that cannot be changed, courage to change the things that can be changed and wisdom to distinguish one from the other." To overcome these obstacles, I had to focus on the elements of the business that I could control.

I had to focus on successfully building the business, but, initially, take only baby steps. In my industry, you need artists, engineers, and designers to do just about anything. Business people, such as I, are then needed to make something fiscally successful. While I had no design training or professional experience, I set about using my knowledge of the industry to design our first product. I was also able to make progress on creating the business plan, model and the concepts that would ultimately make **Novel** a viable new venture. We chose the name **Novel** for our company because we are going to change two established industries in a way that has never been attempted before, and that, we believe will have a profound, positive impact on the world. We may well be the next "big thing." Even if our chances are small, though I think they are as high as they can be, without actually being in the arena we would have no chance.

In the beginning, however, progress was painstakingly slow. The resources I needed did not come as quickly or easily as I would have hoped. At many points, I kept going simply because there was nothing else I could do. I was fully committed to learn and to succeed.

I did learn. I learned that entrepreneurship is not linear especially with younger entrepreneurs. It is exponential. You have to crawl before you can limp; limp before you can walk; walk before you can jog, and jog before you can run. With an exponential curve, progress is slow at the onset. I learned that this slow progress is the reason why most people give up on entrepreneurship. The first part of the process, before the company has legs, often does not look like success. Instead, it looks like exactly what it is, a long, emotional, trying and character-building journey. Here is where most entrepreneurs end the journey.

However, if entrepreneurs continue the journey beyond the risk and the downside, they will understand what I now understand. The downside and risk are dwarfed by the upside and energy. I now love what I do each minute of each day. I guess I always loved what I did even during the worst times because I believed in my success.

Novel, Inc. is now venture capital funded. I have a team of twenty, and the company has created twelve jobs in its first year since incorporation. I cannot imagine working with a better group of people who each in his/her own way inspires me in different ways every day. We now have the experience, talent, intelligence and ambition onboard to successfully launch the company and our products. We, together, experience a job where we do what we love every day, and the future is constantly getting brighter.

In writing this chapter, I was asked to discuss the outcomes of taking the risk to become an entrepreneur. I would strongly caution those who are getting into entrepreneurship for the external consequences of wealth or fame. Those motivations are not strong enough to carry you through the tough times. If, however, your internal motivations are to create something great, to make the world better, and if you cannot see yourself doing anything else, then the external rewards will follow. For example, I have the opportunity of leading a terrific team of creative professionals; I do not worry about money in the future, and I feel that if I desired to, I could retire before the age of thirty. However, I have no desire to ever retire because my work is a passion.

Because of the risks I had to take as an entrepreneur, This last month I had the opportunity attend a Presidential Summit in Washington, D.C. with a friend of mine who was a delegate from Saudi Arabia. I then attended a Global Leadership Conference with Entrepreneur's Organization in New Orleans. Soon, I will be in New York to attend the World Innovation Forum backstage, and in the near future I will be one of a few representatives for young entrepreneurship for the United States at the G20 Summit in Toronto. If I had not taken risks, none of this would have been possible. I would not have any of these relationships or opportunities.

In addition, our company has been featured in *The New York Times, Business Week,* and has been the recipient of multiple accolades and global awards. We were selected by *Entrepreneur's Organization,* from 1,500 competitive businesses across thirty-three countries, as one of the top thirty student age entrepreneurs in the world. In this same competition, **Novel** also received the *Pacific Northwest Innovation Award* from *Microsoft* due to our orientation and strategy that will revolutionize the video game industry.

We are poised to do something incredible this coming year, and we believe the launch of our first two products will not just change the videogame industry, but it will impact the business world at large. We are already in talks with a handful of major Fortune 500 companies, and have not yet even launched our product.

I have shared my story, now, I offer you this advice. Even if you accept the belief that all businesses are created equal, and you can do nothing to alter your chance of success, notions I do not accept, then, you still have a 20% chance of success. These are still better than your odds of being equally successful in a career job. However, this next observation is a certainty. Unless you try, your odds of building a successful business remain at absolutely 0% .Worse still, you will never know a life where you had the opportunity to dare greatly and to experience the rewards of risk:

The credit belongs to the man who is actually in the arena, whose face is marred by dust and sweat and blood, who strives valiantly, who errs and comes up short again and again, because there is no effort without error or shortcoming, but who knows the great enthusiasms, the great devotions, who spends himself for a worthy cause; who, at the best, knows, in the end, the triumph of high achievement, and who, at the worst, if he fails, at least he fails while daring greatly, so that his place shall never be with those cold and timid souls who knew neither victory nor defeat.

—Theodore Roosevelt

Notes

1. http://techcrunch.com/2007/11/14/entrepreneur-20/

2. http://en.wikipedia.org/wiki/Venture_capital

Turning Risk Into Reward

WILL ROSELLINI

I don't take business risks; I control them.

—HENRY FORD

A former professional athlete and an accomplished academic, Will Rosellini is the driving force behind a medical device company that is positioned to revolutionize the way patients manage chronic pain as well as a number of other neurological symptoms. The device based on wireless neurostimulation has gained wide-spread attention under Will Rosellini's direction as founder and CEO of the company.

Will Rosellini's entrepreneurial spirit coupled with his desire to understand the complexities of running a company pushed him to pursue academic degrees in the academic areas which would insure his business success. He has been awarded an MBA, a JD, an MS in Accounting, an MS in Computational Biology, a Master of Regulatory Science, and an MS in Neuroscience. Currently, he is a candidate for a PhD in Neuroscience.

His expertise prompted Congress to invite him to testify about the status of public-private financing for neurotechnology. In addition to sharing his expertise and knowledge in this area with Congress, Mr. Rosellini has conducted interviews with *Newsweek*, *The BusinessMakers*, the *Washington Business Journal*, the *MIT Technology Review Journal*, and *CNN Money*.

It may be difficult to believe, but it is accurate to state that often when in a position of having to make certain crucial business decisions, a CEO may have access to less than 10% of the information necessary to assure him of making a "fool proof" business decision. This limitation exposes both the CEO and the business he/she runs to significant risk and dilemma. Making an incorrect decision could potentially cripple the business. On the other hand, waiting for 100% accurate information and assurance before making a decision, could result in a business that loses its relevance in the market place. What is the most advisable course of action? The majority of entrepreneurs who have experienced such a dilemma would offer this advice, "Risk making the mistake." I would agree, but I would also suggest that the risk is not in making the mistake; the risk is in failing to recognize the mistake(s) as being the vehicle to greater business success. I have discovered that the only way to find out what is wrong with my business is to, in my words, "break it." Lesson learned. Presently, I view my job in my business as being to embrace the mistakes and push those mistakes "to break my business."

I didn't always understand this process, nor was it necessary for me to do so. I was once a blue-chip prospect baseball player. I played on Team USA in the Olympics, competed in the College World Series and was drafted by the Arizona Diamondbacks. Through these steps, my intense preparation focused on one goal: perfection on the baseball diamond. However, this preparation and my goal were not enough. At the age of twenty-two, after nearly ten years of preparing for my dream, I came to the realization that I would not be a regular starter in the arena of professional base-ball. To me, this realization also meant that I failed. I was twenty-two, but I felt that my life was over.

Or so I thought.

Just as I came to the realization that I would never be a regular starter in the pro baseball arena, I came to the realization that I still possessed the same work ethic that had driven me so intensely. Immedi-ately, I began to think about the venture that would next engage me. At this time, I had the freedom to do whatever I wanted...I was a washed up baseball player, and people's expectations for me were very low; how-ever, my expectations for myself were not. My attitude toward new experiences and my high expectations for myself gave me the confidence to try new adventures and to allow myself to fail again...

With the newfound freedom, I began to pursue a subject that had intrigued me as an athlete, neurology, more, specifically, operating a damaged nervous system by computer stimulation. I began to read intently about the *DARPA Revolutionizing Prosthetics Program,* and, the more I read, the more I became certain that I wanted to be involved in this exciting new field.

In 2002, I first began my journey by evaluating my business talents and academic background. I knew that I would be required to read and to comprehend a broad range of scientific papers and studies in order to understand this neurological frontier. In addition, if I wanted to become involved in the business end of this venture, I needed to develop an expertise in understanding the potential market, the strategies of bringing this invention to this market, and the financial dynamics of running a business that would serve this market.

Becoming proficient in these skills necessitated my furthering my education. It also meant that I would run my first risk—the possibility of failing a necessary course of study. I anticipated this risk, and I had a strategy and a goal. My strategy in juggling academic hours demanded that I take my law courses in Long Island in the morning, and commute two hours in order to take science courses in New Jersey's NJIT at night. This strategy together with other creative maneuvers allowed me to complete a demanding sixty-four hours of science and legal coursework in one calendar year. My goal was to become competent in these subjects and to transfer this competence to my entrepreneurial endeavors.

I continued my academic studies after a transfer to the University of Houston where I continued advanced studies on the legal issues surrounding neuroprosthetic rights. All of that said, I have completed 222 hours of graduate coursework, and I expect to complete an additional 132 hours on a part-time basis in the next three years. My academic achievements were possible because I accepted the fact that sometimes I would not have the right answer; other times, I would fail a test. It also meant that by speeding up the mistakes I was making, I was also learning from them at a rate that was much faster than I could previously imagine. In fact, I had come to understand that it is more significant in one's experience to make a hundred mistakes rapidly than it is to make one correct choice deliberately.

I applied this fast fail philosophy to my second start-up company, **MicroTransponder, Incorporated. MicroTransponder ,Inc.** (MTI) is in the process of developing a wireless neurostimulation system, *MicroStim™ System,* for the treatment of chronic pain and several other neurological indications. The system will provide relief from chronic pain without requiring an implanted battery or wires. Its implantable stimulator is the size of two grains of rice and is wirelessly powered via an external controller. The small form factor of the device greatly increases the number of treatment areas. It also makes the implanting procedure minimally invasive and less traumatic for the patient than the procedure is with competing devices.

Since its founding in 2006, **MicroTransponder, Inc.** has raised $17 million to develop its wireless neurostimulation device. In addition to private funding, MicroTransponder has received an award from the

Texas Emerging Technology Fund and eight *NIH SBIR* grants. These grant awards demonstrate a strong independent validation from the scientific community.

The initial success of **MicroTransponder, Inc.** is based on a core group of ideals which encourages the generation of ideas, the exchange of heated debates, and the openness of making mistakes. While it is okay to be wrong, it is important to be wrong very fast in order to glean the knowledge and compute the data from that mistake. The risk involved in making the mistake is controlled by "failing fast."

It has been eight years since I retired from professional baseball, and, now, because of hard work, determination, creative thinking, and, most importantly, because of making mistakes, I am no longer viewed as the failed baseball player, I am applauded as the successful and accomplished scientist.

Turning Risk Into Reward

JAMIE XUEREB

Two to three nights a week throughout my childhood, I would help my parents in their cleaning business. My task was to go into each office to collect all of the rubbish from bins and place the rubbish into a garbage bag. I have many memories of my nights helping my parents, but one memory touched me deeply. One night as I was picking up the rubbish in one of the offices, a grown man was still sitting at his executive desk. Tears were running down his face. I picked up his rubbish, and I left his office. Later that night my parents explained to me the risks of going into business, and then, they explained that we would no longer clean the office of the man who had been crying. He had lost his business in a failed business venture. I have taken that memory with me as I began my own entrepreneurial journey.

About ten years ago, I was in my final year in high school. As most high school seniors, I needed extra money, so I had a job working in a bottle cap factory. Besides motivating me to get a better academic score to get into a university degree, the job also provided me with extra cash. My older brother had a more adventurous spirit, and he had a plan that could make us more money. Being the younger brother, I was persuaded by my only sibling Jason to pool our money to buy a sticker cutting machine from eBay. The cost of the machine was $500. Our plan was simple; we would make stickers only for family and friends. As we planned this business venture, we thought we were very "cool."

My brother and I purchased the sticker machine, and we started doing the odd sticker jobs for family and friends. Once I finished school, we began getting a couple of jobs a week. Then, business took a turn.

My mother Rita referred a friend to us. For some reason, this friend needed her whole store covered with stickers. At the time we thought this was a really big job, and we enthusiastically went to work. In the middle of this job, our cutting machine broke down, so it was time to upgrade. It was also the time that Jason and I believed we could make a viable venture out of this market.

With this idea in mind, we went shopping for a new sticker cutting machine. In our searches we found a machine which could print stickers as well as cut them. However, the machine that could do it all was $20,000. This price was $17,000 out of our price range. For that sort of money we would need financing, and we knew that no financial institution would loan two young men who had no business history or assets that amount of money.

However my father liked what he saw. He thought there was potential with such a machine. He also believed that we were serious about getting into business. He would have hoped that we would take control of his cleaning business eventually, but what he realized was that it was easier to systemize a business such as ours then it was with his cleaning business. My father backed us 100% and declared that he would guarantor us for a loan. It seemed as though we were well into our business adventure.

At this time, we realized our first limitation. For months all we had done was cut stickers, and we had no current work for sticker printing. So, before we went through with purchasing the machine, we did some planning and crunched some figures. We knew that purchasing the machine would give our business some direction by becoming digital printers. We also knew in the first year of having the machine we would not have much print work as this was not the original market that we targeted. However, in our second and third years we would see growth in our printing production.

Next, because of the backing of our parents, getting financing was very easy. Yet, as a business grows, logistical problems arise. At this stage we had taken over three rooms of our parents' home, and we had reason to believe we would get even more cramped.

When the printer was delivered to our house, we had no forklifts, and we were in a suburban area. How would we move the machine? That problem was solved when we sought the help of some friends to hand carry our 200 kilogram gigantic printer off of a truck and into the house.

After six months, our business was growing slowly. It took this amount of time for us to go through one ink cartridge. To anyone who knows the printing business, this pace defines SLOW. To put this into perspective, at this point in our business we go through the same amount of ink in two days. Still, we had ambitions to grow, and we knew to do this we would need a place of our own. Our search for office space that suited our needs began in ernest.

At the same time, we also needed more equipment. The way we would obtain the necessary equipment is by bootstrapping. In order to provide cash flow for our business, we would take on work even though we were not suited for them. For example, Jason and I worked for 24 hours straight on an installation job outdoors. We had to remove some graphics off of vehicles. We worked through the night at freezing temperatures, and our fingers were bleeding by the end of the job. However, because of this job we were able to buy a laminator which is vital to our business now.

At the end of 2007, we moved our company into an oversized factory, and this is when **Mediapoint** was really born. By this time, we knew exactly who we were and what we did. The space we were in meant we had all the room we needed to grow **Mediapoint** and to explore viable ideas for growth and opportunities. However, the cost of renting the space meant that Jason and I did not receive a salary or money from the business until two years after starting. This restriction would be a sacrifice, but it would assure us of the money we needed for our business to succeed.

Today, **Mediapoint** is a leader in the Australian digital sticker printing market. Our revenue is building each year, and we will crack the one million revenue mark in a couple of years. From our humble beginnings this mark is quite a success. There are other signs of our success and growth,we currently have an additional full time team member. We also now have three bigger, faster printers which have replaced our first printer that was moved into our parents' home.

That risk we took by purchasing our first printer has really truly paid off over the last twelve months. At the early stage of this journey, we were two young kids who were venturing into the unknown. Our success was from hard work and determination. Sure, there were times where we could have easily quit. However, in my heart I knew that I was building something special which would pay dividends in the future.

When I reflect on the risk that we took to begin **Mediapoint**, I am always drawn back to the image of the executive who was crying at his desk. Now, I can understand why he was so upset, and, in the back of my mind, I never want to be that person.

Consequently, it is in my nature and the fabric of who I am to take only managed risks. Because of this caution, Jason and I are conservative in our growth. We know that the quicker we grow is also how quickly everything can be taken from us. At this moment we are concentrating on building solid relationships with our existing clients as well as offering an exceptional service to new customers. In the future we will be adding more workers to our team. However, instead of taking another risk, we want to ensure the business is in a position to be able to have room for another person and not move into the unknown. Our process is to plan our future growth and predict the right time to hire someone to join our team.

Although we have spent a couple of hundred thousand dollars on equipment and capital expenditure, spending this money was not as 'scary' once we knew we had the demand to warrant certain acquisitions. The lesson that our experience can offer is that baby steps are needed before you can walk. Also, remember that you need good balance before you start running, or more than likely, you will fall over.

AFTERWORD

When asked for my thoughts on "Turning Risk into Reward" to include in the 2010 GSEA book, my first reaction was, "What do they mean by reward?" You see, I'm not your classic entrepreneur whose primary focus is on the financial bottom line. Sure, I want to take care of my family, generate income for my employees, and bring business to the community. But first and foremost, the reward for me, and for many young entrepreneurs I've met through EO, is having a social impact. For us, risk is just part of the process to get there.

Re-entering New Orleans in a boat and standing on the roof of my flooded, hurricane-ravaged house in 2005, I realized I was at a tipping point in my life. It was surreal to witness the disaster and tragedy caused by Hurricane Katrina in the city that I love. A television clip just doesn't capture it. From my flooded house in Lakeview, near the 17th Street Canal breach, you could drive for two hours without ever leaving this flooded, lifeless zone—an urban devastation seven times the size of Manhattan. All of my neighbors and most of my employees lost their homes and everything in them. Several of our neighbors and friends, along with 1,836 other people, died from the hurricane's force and flooding.

A couple of years prior to Katrina, my business partner and I had completed renovation of a dilapidated 150-year-old warehouse in mid-city New Orleans, which served as our construction company's headquarters. We painstakingly designed the office to resemble our construction sites in order to display the wide variety of materials we use for projects. We had established Ellis Construction in New Orleans in 1996 and were riding a wave of growth in revenues after diversifying our project load, from restaurants and condominiums only, to residential homes, hotel projects, and office buildings. As a result of that shift in strategy our revenue increased by 48% the first year.

We thought the company's broad base of projects would insulate it from any possible downturn, as we anxiously awaited possible economic scenarios to play out at the local and national levels, as well as a decision on whether the U.S. would declare war on Iraq. Concerned that these events might adversely affect investor decisions, we proactively took steps to try to minimize the risk. Little did we know that none of these perceived risks were going to bring our business to a screeching halt. Instead, the worst natural disaster in U.S. history would pose the greatest threat to our future.

In the aftermath of Katrina, our new offices flooded. Twice we moved our temporary office and worked on folding tables until we were able to rebuild. Six months after the storm, we moved back into our office, still, however, without phone lines or electricity. Fifteen employees were forced to live in trailers in our parking lot for nearly a year.

Some might ask why we would risk rebuilding in New Orleans. Why not just move our company somewhere else? For us, risk wasn't the critical factor and rebuilding our business wasn't a choice. We had 45 employees, and each of those employees had four or more other dependents. Multiply that out and you have 400 to 500 people who depended on our company—and on us. A key characteristic of an entrepreneur is leadership, and leadership is all about risk and adaptability. When we're clear about our purpose, vision, and values, we can manage around the risk.

There are very few examples in history where an entire community stops and then re-starts; but that's exactly what happened in New Orleans. Despite the perceived risk of doing business in the region post-Katrina, entrepreneurship has grown in the New Orleans area with a higher rate of individuals starting businesses in that area than nationally--450 per 100,000 people in the New Orleans region, compared with 320 per 100,000 across the United States.

Some people believe that entrepreneurs like to take risk and are motivated by the excitement that it brings. I believe entrepreneurs tend to be risk-averse. In an analysis of the five key capabilities that make up centered leadership, known as the McKinsey Leadership Project, the authors describe how leaders deal with risk. The McKinsey model refers to this dimension of entrepreneurial capabilities as *engaging:* "pursuing opportunities disguised by risk." Rather than letting risk get in the way of their dreams, entrepreneurs manage risk by creating plans, problem-solving, and thinking critically.

Doug Stern, CEO of United Media, proposes some practical advice on how to deal with risk and build confidence for confronting the unknown. He refers to the process as "risk mitigation strategies." These strategies include:

1. Imagining every possible scenario,
2. Describing each scenario in great detail to identify all possible opportunities and risks, and
3. Developing a plan, if needed, in response to each possible scenario.

The most difficult part for many leaders in regard to dealing with risk is admitting they don't have all the answers. Once fears are faced and plans are in place to deal with the possibilities, people can move forward with confidence.

Though the rebuilding of New Orleans is slow and painful, like so many other entrepreneurs, I refuse to be a victim. Somehow, what might have been a crippling blow to our morale and ability to function actually brought out the best in us. It showed us, without question, that our future success is ultimately a result of our mindset and attitude. Katrina didn't cause the problems, it simply exposed them and revealed, in an unprecedented way, the opportunities that exist all around us to help people and to meet societal needs.

Entrepreneurs are known for creating jobs and stimulating economic growth. In reality, we have a much greater role—and from my perspective a much more important one—of impacting society. Since Katrina, I've seen first-hand how entrepreneurship is helping break the cycles of poverty, homelessness, and hopelessness in my community.

What do entrepreneurs do? Some have dreams and pursue them for personal success, but it doesn't end there. Entrepreneurs create new jobs and innovations that fuel the world's economy. We have the power not only to revive the New Orleans area but to revive economies and communities around the globe. Even before the floodwaters subsided, the members of EO New Orleans were picking up the pieces of their lives, the lives of their employees, and their communities. They did not wait for the bureaucracy to begin rebuilding their lives. They adapted, innovated, and moved quickly to begin the rebuilding.

My fellow EO New Orleans member Marshall Klein, who has since passed away, shared with us a profound realization he had before his death. In the months before he died, he expressed that he had found clarity of purpose. He discovered that true fulfillment only comes with life balance and the selfless sharing of knowledge with other entrepreneurs as they strive to realize their dreams. He challenged that we each find our own purpose, with clarity, and pursue it wholeheartedly.

After Katrina, despite the suffering and difficulties around me, I found this clarity, along with many others in my chapter. We saw the power that our dreams, though we had pursued them individually, had on a great number of people. We realized that every community, if it is filled with highly skilled entrepreneurs, can transform the economy of its region. We felt fully the vision of EO—to build the world's most influential community of entrepreneurs—and the importance of that vision beyond the organization. We made it our goal to help entrepreneurs overcome the grave challenges threatening their businesses and prosper. We recognized that New Orleans was originally built by entrepreneurs and would now be rebuilt by entrepreneurs.

It might seem that we had little to give in the months following Katrina, but the truth is that we still had what mattered: time and talent. Though money matters, it is knowledge that truly transforms lives. So we decided to share our hard-earned knowledge and expertise with entrepreneurs at every stage of development by participating in the EO Accelerator Program.

On Thursday, 2 November 2006, a little more than a year after the storm, our chapter held the largest event in our history to launch the EO Accelerator Program. It was truly a moving, rewarding, and exciting experience to see so many members from our chapter step up, embrace the program, and get involved. Even better, it was a home run with the participants.

I won't go into details about the program, because it's one of those things I'm so passionate about that I could fill a library. But I will tell you that it's essentially about mentoring, in its simplest form—a connection between individuals, one entrepreneur learning from other entrepreneurs. Though it's just getting started, I see myself in the participants. When they show up, eager to learn and know and grow, I can't help but be moved, knowing that we, as people and as entrepreneurs, are really fighting for the same thing.

I recently returned with renewed fervor from three weeks of traveling with a delegation of entrepreneurs from 28 different countries. Our goal was to achieve cross-cultural understanding and to help support entrepreneurs in other countries. Some people may wonder why I would want to help entrepreneurs in other countries. One young female entrepreneur from Egypt, whom I met through my work with EO, explained the rationale better than I could in a long-winded philosophical answer, when she shared her goal as an entrepreneur—to impact one million young women back home.

In this year's GSEA competition, I was moved by the story of Milun, a Canadian immigrant from Bosnia. Milun won the 2009 competition because of his persistence and his way of inspiring other students. Milun struck a chord with me when he shared some of his background and what he learned from it—"how important it is to really look out for one another." I get what these young people are doing. Their passion demonstrates the potential we have, individually and collectively, as entrepreneurs. Our potential is unleashed through EO's ambition to stimulate the economy, foster job growth, and encourage entrepreneurship *in all corners of the world.*

Sometimes, when we are in a comfort zone, we miss the big picture. Katrina helped us clear our minds of all the unimportant clutter. It brought to light for many people the importance of focusing on what really matters—family, friends, giving back, and a sense of community. One of my greatest rewards from being an entrepreneur is the opportunity to give back, including my work with EO. It's really a win/win situation. I may be giving my time and talent, asking for nothing in return, but chances are, like it or not, I am going to receive in unexpected ways much more benefit as a result of my actions to reach out to others in need.

Entrepreneurship is about pursuing dreams by overcoming adversity. We all have an end. We can't live forever. But when we find clarity of purpose, we can give that purpose life and it will continue long after we are gone. The entrepreneur's dream never has to end.

—KEVIN LANGLEY
Chairman Elect, Entrepreneurs' Organization
CEO, Ellis Construction, Inc.